Cal Ripken Jr.

PHOTO CREDITS
Bernstein Assoc. Inc.
Jon Soohoo: Cover, pg. 2, 3, 6, 9, 10, 13, 14, 17, 18, 21, 22, 25, 26 and 29
Art Foxall: pg. 30

Distributed to Schools and Libraries
in the United States by
ENCYCLOPAEDIA BRITANNICA EDUCATIONAL CORP.
310 S. Michigan Avenue
Chicago, Illinois 60604

Library of Congress Cataloging-in-Publication Data
Rambeck, Richard.
Cal Ripken, Jr. / by Richard Rambeck.
p. cm.
Summary: A biography of record-setting shortstop, Cal Ripken, Jr.
ISBN 0-89565-867-4
1. Ripken, Cal, 1960-   —Juvenile literature.
2. Baseball players–United States–Biography–Juvenile literature.
3. Shortstop (Baseball)–Juvenile literature.
[1. Ripkin, Cal, 1960-   . 2. Baseball players.]
I. Title.
GV865.R47R36 1993   91-46590
796.357′092–dc20   CIP
[B]   AC

Cal Ripken Jr.

by Richard Rambeck

Cal Ripken's home run swing.

The day before the 1991 All-Star Game, there was a contest. A home run hitting contest in Toronto's Skydome Stadium, the same place the All-Star Game was played the next day. All the top sluggers in Major League Baseball took part in the contest. Cecil Fielder of the Detroit Tigers. Jose Canseco of the Oakland A's. Joe Carter of the Toronto Blue Jays. Howard Johnson of the New York Mets. But on this day, there was one slugger who stood the tallest. Cal Ripken Jr. of the Baltimore Orioles.

During his career, Ripken had always been a good hitter with some power. He hit at least twenty homers in nine straight seasons. Cal, however, had never had more than twenty-eight in a year. But this was 1991, and nobody was swinging a hotter bat than Cal Ripken Jr. As Ripken stepped into the batter's box in the home run contest, there was a buzz in the crowd. He was leading the American League in hitting. Ripken also was having the best year of his great career. Something special was going to happen.

In the contest, Ripken faced twenty-two pitches. He slammed twelve of them – TWELVE! – over the Skydome fences. Nobody else in the contest hit nearly that many home runs. Afterward, Ripken just shrugged his shoulders when asked about what he had done. "I'm not really sure what happened," he admitted. "I just felt good today." He must have felt good the next day, too. In his first time at bat in the All-Star Game, Ripken slugged a three-run homer. He was named Most Valuable Player of the game as his American League team won 4-2.

After the All-Star Game, Ripken kept up the hot hitting. He completed the best season of his career by hitting thirty-four home runs. He drove in 114 runs. And he wound up hitting .323, which was sixth best in the American League. His homers, runs batted in, and batting average were all career highs. At the end of the 1991 season, many experts were calling Ripken the best player in the major leagues. That was kind of strange, because a year before many of those experts said Ripken was washed up.

During the 1990 season, Cal Ripken Jr. had a batting average of .250. It was his worst year ever. The Baltimore fans began to think there was something wrong with Ripken. But what? Well, some people said, maybe he was tired. After all, Ripken hadn't missed a game in almost nine years. Every day, game after game, Cal Ripken Jr. was Baltimore's starting shortstop. He had played in almost 1,500 straight games. Only New York Yankee great Lou Gehrig had gone longer without missing a game.

Ripken, however, didn't want to rest. He wanted to play every day. Always has, always will. "I've never heard him say, 'I'm not feeling so good today,'" said Baltimore first baseman Randy Milligan. "I say that <u>every</u> day." Ripken, though, wasn't feeling good about his hitting after the 1990 season. During the offseason, Ripken worked every day on improving his swing. "I got away from what made me successful," Ripken explained. He wound up changing almost everything. The way he stood at the plate. How he held the bat. Everything.

17

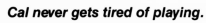

When the 1991 season started, Ripken was a new man. "This year I've gotten things more in focus," he said. "And it's taken away any doubts." Given how good Ripken had been for so many years, it's amazing anyone doubted the Baltimore superstar. His whole life had been about becoming a major league baseball player. His father, Cal Ripken Sr., was a coach for the Orioles before Cal Jr. was even born. Cal Jr. grew up around Baltimore players and coaches.

As a kid, he would often ride with his father to Oriole practices. "When Dad first asked if I wanted to go to the ballpark with him, I went because I could be with him alone on the drive there and back," Ripken said. "Soon I began to enjoy baseball." Cal Jr. also began to learn baseball. He would ask some of the Baltimore stars for tips on how to play. When the players gave Cal Jr. advice, the youngster would go back and tell his father what they said. "My dad was always the final authority," Cal Jr. explained. "If he told me the guy gave me correct information, I knew I could go back to him."

When Cal Jr. joined the Orioles in 1981, it became impossible to move him out of the starting lineup. Ripken never missed an inning, let alone a game, during his first few years in the major leagues. In 1982, he was named American League Rookie of the Year after hitting twenty-eight home runs and driving in ninety-three runs. A year later, he was even better. Ripken batted .318, hit twenty-seven homers, and had 102 RBIs. He was named American League Most Valuable Player. Led by Ripken and first baseman Eddie Murray, the Orioles won the American League pennant and the World Series.

Young Cal Ripken had become one
of the top players in the game. But he
wasn't about to let success go to his head.
Every time Ripken went on the field, he
tried to give his best. That's because he
hated to lose. In fact, he hated to lose at
anything. "I grew up in a family where
everything was a competition," Ripken said.
"Everything you did, it was fun. You did
well. You tried hard. If you didn't, it wasn't
fun." When Cal Jr. became an adult, he still
tried as hard as he could no matter what.

During spring training, the Orioles have their players take a twelve minute run. "You don't have to try," explains Baltimore outfielder Brady Anderson. "He [Ripken] tries. He comes to me before the race and plans out how we're going to run it." In 1990, Anderson finished first in the run. For once, Ripken didn't win, and Cal was not happy about it. "He got mad at me," Anderson said of Ripken. "He said I went out too fast, that I broke him down." Baltimore manager John Oates likes to tell another story about Ripken.

"**C**al had gone two games without a hit," Oates recalled during the 1991 season. "So he wanted to take extra hitting practice. He hasn't missed a batting practice in ten years. Early hitting takes an hour. So I tell him to come out for just the last fifteen minutes and hit." Ripken, however, was there when the hitting practice began. The next thing Oates sees is Ripken and Baltimore outfielder Tim Hulett climbing the outfield fence. They're playing a game. They're trying to swat batting practice homers back into the ballpark.

Cal waits for the pitch.

No errors for ninety-five games.

When Ripken's not trying to rob teammates of home runs in practice, he's playing errorless ball at shortstop. He made only three errors all season in 1990. In fact, he went ninety-five games without an error that year, a major league record for a shortstop. That's just one of many records Ripken holds. Before his career ends, he will set many more. Ripken is a sure bet to make it to baseball's Hall of Fame. But no matter what happens to him, Cal Ripken Jr. will always try as hard as he can. It's the only way he knows how to play.

Date Due

AUG 2 7 '97		
DEC 2 9 '97		
MAY 2 7 '98		
SEP 0 4 2001		
OCT 0 7 2008		